Dirty Laundry

Confessions of an Escort A

Michael Robinson

About the Author

Mike Robinson had a difficult childhood and was diagnosed with schizoaffective disorder at the age of 17.

At the age of 20, Robinson joined the 4th Battalion Parachute Regiment, and later the 3rd Battalion Prince of Wales's Own Regiment. Upon passing out, he was awarded 'most improved recruit'.

Later into his military career, Robinson volunteered for the arduous 'Cambrian Patrol', a type of special forces training, with a view to joining the SAS. However, during deployment in the Breacon Beacons, Robinson succumbed to hypothermia, and was ultimately sacked from the Army on Christmas Eve after they looked into his medical records.

From here, Robinson ended up in HM Prison Hull and later locked up indefinitely under Section 37/41. He remained locked up for about three years and on his release wrote about his experiences in his autobiography Sectioned: The Book the NHS Tried to Ban on Amazon Kindle.

As well as a soldier, other jobs Robinson has done include drummer for two successful groups, carer at a special needs school, chef, bouncer, driver and minder for a Hull escort agency. Also, he has an NVQ in catering, a diploma in Uniform Public Services, and has read law with criminology at university.

Robinson has been married to his long term partner, Julie, for six years. He continues to support mental health campaigns with the help of his local MP and other government agencies. This includes working with the Heads Together campaign, Mind, and other mental health charities.

(You Tube: "heads together campaign michael 'robbo' robinson")

He regularly helps out the homeless in Hull and other persons/groups in need where he can.

In 2019 Robinson published his first novel "The Killing Moon" with a view to it being made into a film.

Prologue

Today, I spent the last three hours filling in yet another job application form. The reason it took three hours is because of my dyslexia. The vacancy, I know full well, I won't get. It was a pointless and fruitless exercise, but one that I undertake regularly. However controversial this sounds, I am not gay, I am not transsexual, I do not come from an ethnic minority background, I'm not Polish and I am not a woman. I do, however, have schizoaffective disorder, a form of schizophrenia. What do all the above have which I do not? All have rights enshrined in British law. As a service user, I do not have any of the rights these so-called minority groups have access to. If I did, then chances are I'd be employed.

There was, however, one job that I did for around 18 months. I was a minder/driver for an escort agency in Hull. I was not taken on because of these rights that were mentioned, I was taken on merit. I had a choice to make. Do I remain in the benefits system, constantly in debt, being lucky if I eat one meal a day, with no prospects and the endless monotony of filling in job application forms for jobs that I'll never aspire to; or, I could make some quick, fast danger money. Anyone who has ever lived on benefits will understand the desperation that comes from living on money from the state. I had a car, I had my build and I had my wits. Above all, I had respect for the ladies I worked with. This is their story as well as mine.

I must make clear from the beginning, despite the book's title, I'm going to give nothing away regarding the identities of those I worked with. All of the names I refer to are pseudonyms to protect the girls whose job it is to keep the clients happy. Also, some of the addresses and locations have been altered, again, not to protect the client base per se, but more to protect the anonymity of the girls. I am not particularly bothered about repercussions from other areas such as the underworld, for which I worked. I'm sure they've got enough problems of their own to deal with and as it becomes apparent in the book, I can look after myself.

As for the girls I worked with, various girls got in the business for various reasons. For some, it was a means to an end, particularly if they had young families. The benefits system, under the Tory regime, meant these girls were given less than the bare minimum to live on. As a result, they were forced into this line of work. Others were quite clearly dependent on drugs. Theirs is a story of nothing but tragedy. There were other girls who particularly enjoyed the job. Not only the sex side of it, and the thrill of having a double life, but also interacting with the client base.

Lastly, there were the girls who I particularly respected. The ones who used escorting in order to put themselves through education and university. These girls were tough. They would escort during the night and during the day would work hard in order to leave university or college without debt. They were dependent on no man, and only had themselves to answer to. True fighters. And, in an age where feminism and most feminists are feminazis, hating anything that wasn't in their interests, the girls I worked with showed what it really means to go out and fight for equality and for the respect they earned.

Dedications

This book is dedicated to The Boss. You gave me work when the rest of society would not. It was fun while it lasted.

Much love and respect,

Robbo

Chapter 1

It was about half past one, Saturday morning, when I got the call. I was literally just getting into bed with my wife when The Boss rang. At first, I didn't answer, but then she rang again. I went downstairs to get a coffee and then answered the phone.

"Robbo, can you do me a favour?" said The Boss. "Can you pick up a girl from Hessle and take her to Hornsea? It's an easy job. It's just an hour, but you'll get thirty quid for it."

My mind was racing. Being schizoaffective meant I was permanently paranoid. Was this a set-up to get me filled in? Were drugs involved? Was this a ploy to get me out the house so I could be burgled? Reality took over. I had not really earned any money since I left my last band, The Fixers.

When the band broke, it was a bit like an ugly divorce. Even to this day, the group will still have nothing to do with me. But that was beside the point. The point was, it was thirty quid for just over an hour's work. Fuck it. I'll take the chance. If it was a set-up, I'd just have to fight and learn from my mistakes. If it wasn't, I could put fuel in my car and possibly get a takeaway tomorrow night. The pros seemed to outweigh the cons.

Twenty minutes later, I was in the Co-op car park waiting for a girl whom I'd never met before. 'Who was she?' I wondered, 'Was she a druggy? Was she about 50, overweight and ugly?'

The phone rang. It was The Boss. "Is she there yet?"

"No." I replied, "I've been here 20 minutes, there's no sign of her."

In a cockney accent, The Boss replied "For fuck's sake, hang on, I'll call you back," and then she hung up.

Ten minutes later and my first job had arrived. She was blonde, about 25, quite a stunner, and very thin. I didn't know what to say as she opened the back door of the car and got in behind me. Her working name was Ella. It was obvious The Boss had given her a right telling off down the phone. She seemed pissed off. I put the car into first and started to make my way to Hornsea, all the time, my mind racing. 'Am I in danger? Am I in danger?'

It was obvious Ella didn't want to make conversation. Not that she was rude, it was just she had a job to do and she was probably gearing herself up to do it. To lighten the mood in the car, I turned on the radio. Hewey Morgan, the singer from the Fun Loving Criminals was the DJ. In a deep New York voice he said "Ok, it's time for the Led." and with that, the next song was 'Over the hills, and far away' by Led Zepplin. The drums on the record sounded great as we drove along toward the east-coast village of Hornsea.

My mind began to relax. Maybe this was cut and dry. It was easy money and not a good kicking. It soon dawned on me: I did not know the address of the client. It was times like this I could have used a sat-nav. I turned the radio down and asked Ella "Do you know where this job is? Have you been there before?"

"Yeah I've been before, but I don't know how to get there. However, if you've got the postcode, I can use the sat-nav on my phone."

As we were driving, The Boss rang.

"Robbo, are you there yet? The client's ringing up."

"I'm just coming into Hornsea now, boss. I'll be there in five/ten minutes."

We found the job, although it took us a bit longer. I noticed we'd passed the police station, and again my mind began to race. We stopped at a side street which looked like it had houses on one side and flats on the other. The flats looked like old council flats and it was a bit unusual given they were right opposite what looked like new houses. However, the road itself was tiny.

Ella got out of the car and walked straight to the client's house and knocked. I watched her from behind the steering wheel thinking to myself 'What's gonna happen now?' Five minutes had passed and Ella had still not gone in, again the paranoia began to tick over. Ella then began to walk back towards the car. At the same time, The Boss rang.

"What's 'appening, Robbo, the client's said she's still not got there yet."

Ella got in the car and I handed her the phone. I could hear The Boss shout at her. She finished the call and handed me back the phone and smiled. It was the wrong door.

She went back up the stairwell and knocked on the door opposite. I saw her go inside and waited.

Several things ran through my mind. 'Should I move the car?' or 'What happens if Ella needs me and can't find me?' The time was now about 3 o'clock in the morning, and it was a dark stormy night. Again, I waited. Over an hour had passed since Ella had gone into the client. Again, I asked myself: 'What happens now?'

Five minutes after that, I saw the client's door open, and Ella come out. She hurried along to the car, although this time she got into the passenger seat at the front. I drove off straight away before she even got her seat belt on. Ella was happy and more talkative. We stopped at the garage just on the outskirts of Hornsea. Ella wanted some cigs and asked me if I needed anything. Then she gave me the thirty pounds that The Boss had promised.

Soon, we were on our way back to Hessle and this time Ella and I had a good chat, talking about nothing in particular, but it was obvious that Ella felt relaxed in my company. By half past four, I'd dropped her back in the Co-op car park. She had rang The Boss at this point and told her she was going off for the night.

Five minutes later, I was back home, nursing a cup of coffee. In the end, there was no drama. However, I was thirty quid up. That was how it all began.

Chapter 2

It was about 3 o'clock the next day. It was a Saturday afternoon and I was waiting in the ASDA car park on Hessle Road. The boss had text me and asked me to meet her. I vaguely knew what she looked like as I'd known her ex-husband briefly at college before they got divorced. I didn't know what to expect so I decided to get in the car and wait for the call. I found myself in ASDA. All the time asking myself 'What am I getting involved in? How had I got to this stage in my life that my only source of income would be to go for an interview driving call girls around the City.'

The answer was simple. I had no choice. I did have a good career in the military, although that seemed like a hundred years ago now. At the age of seventeen I developed a form of schizophrenia called schizoaffective disorder. Back then, that meant your career choices were very limited indeed. Eventually, I managed to blag an interview with the TA and I joined the 4th Battalion Parachute Regiment. However, I'd been discovered taking my medication and abruptly kicked out of the regiment. I did, however, have the military bug at this point. Therefore, I got my tablet changed to an injection once-per-month and joined an infantry regiment in Hull.

Even on passing out, I won 'Most Improved Recruit', however, my career in the military was short-lived. After about four years' service I volunteered for a type of Special Forces training. I was deployed to the Brecon Beacons in Wales and succumbed to Hypothermia on exercise. The MOD looked into my medical records and again I was dismissed - only this time it was Christmas Eve 2003. Not long after that, I stopped taking my medication in order to continue with my military career as I was advised. As you can imagine, this led to me becoming unwell, and after two terms in prison for assault, I was moved to a psychiatric unit in Hull where I would spend the next two and a half years.

These were two and a half very long years. I was locked up with some of the most dangerous people in the country. Fortunately, I knew how to look after myself. If the military only taught me one thing, it was to be the grey man. Don't get involved in anything. Don't get noticed. If you're gonna get noticed, make sure it's for a positive. Eventually, the hospital had no choice but to let me go. I was free, but I was also skint, with no career prospects. I tried my damndest to rejoin the military. I contacted my local MP several times and I even tried to go down the legal route, all to no avail. Once I even contacted a TV company to see if they would sponsor me going through the all arms commando course with the title of the programme being called "The Schizophrenic Commando."

It wasn't all bad after I had left the hospital. I enrolled in college to do a uniformed public services course and after the first year I won student of the year. However, my history kept me unemployed. How do you explain to an employer I was locked up indefinitely for two years because of a mental condition, but I'm okay now. The one saving grace in my life had been my wife, Julie. At this point, we'd been married for about three years. However, bills still needed paying. The fact was unemployment in Hull and low wages are part and parcel of the town I live in. Anyone with two convictions for violence as well as an indefinite hospital order does not have their name underlined on any CV. If anything, the line goes through your name.

It soon became apparent that I had no income. This is what led me to the ASDA car park. Even if I did this job for the weekend, it would pay the gas bill, or pay the rent.

It was starting to rain when the phone rang.

Chapter 3

Half an hour later I was making my way to the East Hull village where The Boss lived. I pulled up outside her house on the cul-de-sac and it looked a typical suburban environment - not the type of place you would think of necessarily as being the home of the local madame. I was still unsure of what to think as the front door opened and a ferocious Staffy dog came running to my car, followed by The Boss.

"Don't worry Robbo, it just wants to say hello." Here stood The Boss. She was not what one might imagine a madame to look like. She was tall, attractive and well-spoken, albeit with a hint of a cockney accent. What struck me most of all though, was how young she was. Dolled-up she could easily have passed for her twenties, although she was in her forties. She held out her hand and I took it as she introduced herself. However, there was a problem. She wanted to interview me but she was running late, so she asked me if I would give her a lift and she would interview me en route. The Boss's boyfriend lived on the other side of the city. She grabbed her things and we made our way down Hedon Road towards Gipsyville. The Boss then began to explain the do's and don'ts of the job.

Firstly, I had to make sure I always had condoms in the car. Also, I could not ask any details of the jobs. That was solely between the escort and the client. If the escort wanted to talk about the job, then it was up to me whether I continued with the conversation. Most important though, there was never to be any fraternisation between me and any of the girls. However, she added, if I took a shine to a girl, The Boss could arrange it for me to see her for an hour. However, it was to go through The Boss only. She went on to explain that ninety per cent of the customers were people who rebooked. Although most of the jobs were in the city some went far beyond, including Bridlington and Scarborough to the north, York to the west and Lincoln to the south. She went on to explain the further away the job was, the more money I got for the first hour. After this, it was a set fee. Other things that The Boss explained to me were, I wouldn't necessarily have to sit outside the client's home or hotel for the extent of the booking. Certainly, if the clients were known and there were other jobs to do, then - as long as I was back to pick the escort up in time - there was more money to be made.

The Boss also mentioned some of her lieutenants she had working for her. First of all there was Roger. He was the uncle of one of the escorts. Although Roger had been in the army he had left to join Humberside Police, but he found them too corrupt. He had a number of jobs after he left the police force until, eventually, his niece put him in touch with the agency. It was a weird set-up but it was also none of my business. Roger sometimes did the phones as well as some of the driving. Also he lived alone and was dying from cancer. Another one of The Boss's workers was Stephanie. Stephanie was also an older lady and although Stephanie did the occasional escorting job she was mainly there to answer the phones when The Boss was not running them. Lastly, there was Paul. Paul had been her number one driver for a long time, but I could tell as The Boss was speaking that she wasn't very happy with him.

My role within the agency would be to act as the number two driver and I had to look after the girls and to make sure that they got home safely. I asked if I would ever need to do any of the muscle work, meaning would I have to kick doors in to grab a girl out of a situation. The Boss took it on board what I'd said and then replied, "I've been running this company now for twenty years. In that time I can only think of one or possibly two occasions when a client wouldn't let a girl leave." The Boss went on to explain, "When a guy wants to get his rocks off he wants to have a good time and then get on with watching the football, listening to music, or whatever. Any time I've had a problem with a client we block them from sending girls there again. The same goes for the escorts. If they don't want to see a client they don't have to. And," she added, "they don't have to give a reason." I asked her what happened on the two occasions when the client wouldn't let the escort leave. With an evil look in her eye she said, "I went down there the next day at 6 o'clock at night when I knew his wife and kids would be at home. I spent the next half hour shouting at him on his doorstep and letting his wife know exactly what her husband got up to." She added, "I can be a lot more scary than a load of heavies can be at the right time."

Soon I pulled up near where The Boss's boyfriend lived. As she got out she mentioned that she vetted everyone who worked for her and that she interviewed them all personally. Having done a law degree I knew there was no way The Boss could vet me within such a short space of time and then The Boss hinted that she had connections within the police force who did it for her. At the time I took it on the chin as bravado, although I did not doubt that she knew people within the police. As she walked away she said welcome to the company and that she would ring me with a job later, as soon as it came in.

Chapter 4

Within the next couple of hours I got the call to do a couple of jobs. Again, all the time, my mind was racing - what am I getting involved in? What if there's a problem? However, for all of my doubts, nothing materialised which caused me any concern. The only problem that I did have, however, was knowing the location where all the girls lived. Within a few days I'd asked The Boss to send me details of all the girls' addresses. The Boss texted me them all and I did a recce of all their homes. They were spread all over the city. Some lived in the dodgy areas of East Hull. Others lived on the estate of Bransholme - the largest council estate in the city. Others lived in more affluent areas of West Hull. In total there were around 18 escorts on The Boss's books. It took me a full day to recce all of the addresses and I soon realised that I would need a sat-nav to find all of the locations in the city that I needed to be.

Gently, I was getting used to the job, although my wife began to ask questions. I soon realised that I could not carry on acting suspiciously, taking phone calls then going straight out of the door. It wasn't fair on me and it certainly wasn't fair on Julie. Eventually, I would have to come clean.

The phone rang and a job had come in. The escort was Lola and I had to take her to a job in Brough. I made my way to the high-rise flats on Boothferry Estate and picked her up. Lola couldn't have been more than 21 years of age and it soon became obvious that there was a problem. On the way to the job, Lola kept scratching herself and rubbing her arms, although at the time I paid no attention. We got to the job in Brough and the client was a regular - a married man whose wife went away for half the year. However, he was known to ply the girls with powerful home-made red wine. I dropped Lola at the house and rang The Boss to do the "safe and happy". This was to confirm with the office that the escort had left my care and gone into the client's house. At that point it was up to the escort to ring the office to say that she had been paid and more importantly that she was safe and happy. As long as there wasn't a problem, the office would not need to ring me. However, there was a problem, Lola didn't have credit on her phone therefore she couldn't ring the office. It was starting to become apparent as to why. The Boss then rang the client, spoke to Lola, then rang me back in order to tell me to make sure that Lola had got credit on her phone when she came out of the job.

Roughly an hour later I saw Lola staggering up the street. I got out of the car to ask what was wrong. Again, this was not protocol. Every time an escort left the client's home I was supposed to receive a phone call from The Boss to let me know that she was on her way. I managed to help her into my car and then drove to a car park to sort out the money. I asked Lola for mine and The Boss's cut but she only gave me half. I could tell Lola was out of it. I explained again that it wasn't the full amount and also that she needed to get credit on her phone. The Boss rang. Another job had come in. I managed to get the rest of the money and then made my way to drop Lola off back on the Boothferry estate.

On the way back Lola broke down and started to cry. "I'm a filthy smack head" she sobbed, through the tears. She carried on, "I need my smack." I didn't know what my response should be and I wasn't comfortable having a drug addict in my car. She then asked me to take her to her dealer and wait for her, whilst she got her fix. I explained to her that I had another job on and that it wasn't in my remit. Lola then began to kick-off and scream at me. In turn, I put my foot down and tried to get back to the Boothferry Estate as quickly as I could. As I pulled up outside the high-rise flats, I rang The Boss to tell her I was dropping Lola off. The strong red wine that she'd had with the client meant that she was a wreck and that Lola could hardly walk.

Whilst I was on the phone to The Boss, Lola got out of the car and promptly fell down outside the flats. At the same time a lad in his twenties was outside and asked me what I was staring at. All the time this was going on The Boss was telling me on the phone to pick Lola up and to take her inside. I got out of my car and tried my best to pick Lola up, at the same time as this juvenile was asking me what I was fucking well doing here. Also I had to explain to The Boss what was happening. The Boss started telling me that I could not leave one of her girls in the street, and then told me to hand the phone to the kid who was giving me the threats. As I put him on I heard him say, "All right, it's Callum. How are you doing?"

Turned out that The Boss knew him. All the time I'm wondering whether this guy was going to run off with my phone, whether he was going to pull a knife, whether a load more neanderthals were going to turn up - and at the same time I was responsible for Lola. Then I heard Callum say, "Don't worry. I'll take her up to the flat" and as he handed me my phone, in all the panic I dropped it. At this point I was stressed-out-to-fuck.

I watched Callum carry Lola back into the flats and hurried back to my car as both the passenger and driver doors were wide open. I made my way out of the area and pulled up outside the shops in Hessle Square. The phone rang again. It was The Boss, only this time the phone was broken. Every time I answered the call, the line went dead. The Boss then texted me and then I texted back to explain that the phone wasn't working. It was close to midnight now, on a Monday night. Eventually I managed to get the phone working again and I got through to The Boss and Roger. I could hear Roger telling her in the background, "Give him the night off, now". The Boss duly obliged. I began to think "This is not what I signed up for" and I made my way home.

I never worked with Lola again. She was sacked the next day.

Chapter 5

Within a couple of days I'd saved up to buy a cheap sat-nav from Argos. Also, I realised that I was managing to save quite a bit of money. This in turn meant that I wasn't quite as reliant on food-parcels. Slowly, I was beginning to get my debts down. This included a £1,000 overdraft that I had from the bank. Plus, I was able to buy a TV licence. Gradually, I managed to save up some money at the end of the month. Normally, when I was paid by the government, it would be gone within three days and I would have to wait another ten days before I got paid again. Although I was no Alan Sugar or Richard Branson, slowly I was working my way out of poverty. However, to be fair, I was putting the hours in. So much so that I was working seven days a week, from roughly around 6.00 p.m. to whenever the last job finished, which could be as late as seven in the morning.

Around this stage I decided to come clean with Julie as to what I was up to. Julie had come from a middle-class family, including private school, and as you can imagine she was not best pleased with what I told her. However, she also realised that we needed the money. Fortunately, I managed to talk Julie around and I reassured her that I was just the driver, although I failed to mention that I was also a "minder". The main thing for Julie, though, was that I reassured her that I wasn't having an affair and that I was out working. She took it on the chin and told me to be careful.

The phone rang and it was The Boss's lieutenant, Roger. He told me I had a job to do in Market Weighton and I had to pick up Tiffany for an hour. I picked up Tiffany from her flat in Boulevard, off Hessle Road and we made our way to the job. Tiffany was an attractive girl in her late twenties. She told me that her job during the week was a truck driver. We made light conversation and seemed to be getting on well. We found the job in Market Weighton and within an hour we were heading back towards Hull, only this time I felt as if Tiffany was coming on to me. However, I did not respond, knowing full-well that it was more than my job was worth. I dropped her back home and rang Roger to say that I'd cleared for the night. There were no more jobs for that evening and so I went home.

The next day, I received a text from The Boss, basically saying that I was sacked. I could not think why I might have been sacked and, the truth be told, I was annoyed. I rang The Boss straight away. The Boss turned around and said that Tiffany had told her that I was all over her and that I could not work for her any more. I protested my innocence and then tried explaining that it was the other way around. The Boss then informed me that Tiffany was gay. I did not believe this for a second. However, The Boss was adamant that I was sacked, and there was not a lot that I could do about it. I was more mad at myself for spending £50 of my spare money on a sat-nav and although the debts were down, they were in no way clear. I'd done the job for less than a month and I had already been sacked, although through no fault of my own.

Chapter 6

I spent the next couple of weeks getting my affairs in order. At this point I'd managed to put a new band together, called the Jackdaws. We were just going through the motions of rehearsing as often as possible until we could get some proper paid gigs on the circuit.

As for the agency, I just put it down to experience and thought no more of it. That was until late one night I got a text from The Boss. As we were texting one another she told me that it wasn't the worst thing that I could have done as a driver. As I'd calmed down a lot since we last spoke I felt that I did not need to protest my innocence anymore. The fact was, I quite liked the job and it was easy money - even if it was danger money. In the end, The Boss concluded that I could start work for her again the next night.

Soon, I was back to the old ways. Starting on an evening between seven and nine and working right through until the early hours. Even though I was working seven days a week I was enjoying not only the money but also the interaction with the girls. Over the period of the next few months I started to get quite close to Ellie - also, some of the other girls who I worked with. Often, after a job had finished, we would drive out to a twenty-four hour McDonalds waiting for the next job to come in - just drinking coffee and talking about money, sex, politics and religion. One of the girls who I'd regularly do this with was Roxy.

Roxy was, again, in her late twenties and struggling to get by to support the three kids that she had at home. From what I could gather she was on and off with her long-term partner but I did not pry. However, Roxy was studying full-time at Hull College with a view to reading law at university. Again, I grew quite fond of her and we would spend many a night in debates between jobs, around the legality of what we were doing.

Contrary to popular belief, prostitution is not illegal. What is illegal, however, is to solicit sex. This is why The Boss had to be very careful about what she said down the phone when punters would ring.

For example, you could not make it blatantly obvious what was going on. However, you could say how much it was for the hour and add whatever went on between the client and the escort was between consenting adults. The reason for this was in case the police rang up. However, in all my time working for the agency I never suspected the police of ringing once - especially with all of the Tory government cutbacks Humberside Police probably had bigger fish to fry.

Soon, however, not only was I driving but I would get extra money for answering the phones as well - for example if The Boss wanted a night off, or if she had her kids. The way this came about was that the Boss was going to Manchester for the night to see the Libertines play, and she was stopping over. Stephanie was in hospital at the time and could not do the phones. Also, sadly, Roger had died at this point and so that left me to take the calls and then bookings. Soon, not only was I earning money for driving the girls, but also I was getting extra for taking the bookings. In the weekend the Boss went to Manchester, in bookings alone, I earned an extra £50.

Chapter 7

Around this time The Boss took more girls on her books. There was Summer, a hairdresser from East Hull, who was also a fitness fanatic. She had done this type of work before, in a parlour, only to leave when she got a long-term boyfriend. Then there was Angel. Angel was a cockney MILF and had been working the circuit in London earning five times as much as she was making with us. Also, she'd been known to do porn films. However, she was a "salt of the earth" girl and, like everyone else on the books, was just trying to make ends meet. Another new girl who started was Kennedy. Kennedy was in her early twenties and lived in an east coast holiday village, by the sea. Again, Kennedy was attractive as well as open-minded. I took her to her first job, on a Friday night in Hull city centre. The client was a regular. However The Boss told me that as Kennedy was a new girl I would have to wait outside in case there were any problems. It was obvious Kennedy had a mixture of nervousness and excitement before she went up to the flat and I did my best to reassure her that if there was a problem I would be right outside. Also, I reiterated the fact that The Boss had told me specifically to wait for her. She said, "Wish me luck!" and she cheerily hopped out of the car to do the job. An hour later she returned and was quite pleased with herself - so much so that she could not wait to do the next job. Unfortunately, however, her excitement was short-lived. I never took her to her next job. And unfortunately it was difficult for her as the guy asked her to do things and say things to him which were perverse. He asked Kennedy to pretend that she was his daughter and although you do get jobs like this Kennedy was totally freaked out. After the job she decided that it wasn't for her, which was fair enough, so she quit and The Boss got her a taxi home. I felt it was a shame because she was a nice girl. However, The Boss did not always know what the clients were into. Had Kennedy been doing the job for a few months it might not have been so difficult when dealing with deviants.

Another job that was a regular was guy who lived off Beverley Road and his thing was he used to have three large TV screens in his living room and he enjoyed watching porn on all three at the same time, whilst getting a service.

Dealing with sexual deviances was part of the job, but also the rules were no kids, no animals. Other than that, anything went. Despite our unfortunate start, I was still doing jobs with Tiffany. It was late one night when the phone rang. I was told to pick up Tiffany and take her to a job in Withernsea. I still had my reservations about working with her as she got me sacked. Or so I thought. However, later Roxy told me that Tiffany never said anything about me to The Boss. Either way, it was not up for discussion as I picked her up from the Boulevard and drove east to the seaside town of Withernsea. We chatted quite casually on the way there and there were no awkward moments between us. We got to the job and it was about half one in the morning. It was a normal street and given the time it was not surprising there were only a few living room lights on in the various houses.

As normal I manouvered the car in the direction I wanted it to face and Tiffany got out and went to the front door. I noticed there was no light on in the house. However, this did not mean anything as some clients would entertain either upstairs or in the back room. At the same time I rang The Boss to tell her that Tiffany had gone to the job. Five minutes later and Tiffany had still not gone in. I watched her as she approached my car and got inside. She told me to ring The Boss to check the address. I duly obliged and The Boss could not understand as it was a regular who had used us before. I put the phone down as The Boss made the call to the client. He answered and said that he was in the property and didn't hear Tiffany knocking.

This time Tiffany returned to the door. Again, there was no answer and no sign of life inside the house. Tiffany returned to the car once more, only this time one of the neighbours came out and asked us both what we were doing. She was a fat woman in her 50's with glasses and it was obvious that she was the local busy body. Again, I went through the same rigmarole ringing The Boss and, again, The Boss said she would ring the client. In the meantime, Tiffany explained to the busybody that we had some jewellery to sell on Ebay and we were just delivering. The busybody in return took great pleasure to inform us that he had moved out three weeks ago and that the house was empty. We thanked Mrs. Busybody in order to get rid of her and at the same time The Boss rang to say the client wasn't answering his phone anymore.

The upshot was, it was a hoax call and that we should both return to Hull and have the evening off - although by this time it was two in the morning. On the way back Tiffany and I discussed the job and Tiffany's conclusions were that the client probably had a beef with The Boss and it was his way of getting one back on her.

Again, hoax calls were sometimes in the nature of the beast. Every couple of months we would get a call for a job that amounted to nothing. Most of the time you could tell if they were hoaxes or not. But given the amount of money we were making it just went with the territory. It wasn't long before I dropped Tiffany home and I made my way back home to Hessle.

Chapter 8

Although I had to come clean with Julie about what I was doing, I had to come clean with other people also. I told my mother and ultimately she was fine with it. Mum had worked as a criminal lawyer for the best part of 25 years and because of this she knew some of the most dangerous criminals not only in Hull and Yorkshire but also across the country - including London and Liverpool. Mum knew I could handle myself in a tricky situation and although it wasn't her preferred choice of work for her favourite son, she also knew that I was desperate for the money. Mum probably had an influence regarding my outlook to the criminal fraternity. In other words, I knew how they thought. I maybe didn't have the insight that my mother had. However, most career criminals have the good sense to keep out of the limelight. The days of Ronnie and Reggie Kray being celebrity gangsters are long gone. Most career criminals that are successful do not brag on Facebook about how much money they have. In fact it's quite the opposite. They do not want any attention, unlike some of the junior criminals who welcome the notoriety which ultimately leads to their downfall.

I also told my sister Nicola what I was doing. Generally, as a rule, my sister and I never got on. So it was unsurprising when she took the sanctimonious moral high ground. It didn't bother me what she thought because I wouldn't speak to her for another 3 years anyway.

Another person I had to come clean with was my consultant psychiatrist. As I mentioned earlier, I was placed under a section 37/41. This meant in layman's terms that I was out on license. If I was to get into any bother or even be arrested, in theory, I could be recalled back to the Humber Centre and this would be for an indefinite period. This wouldn't necessarily mean the doctor would recall me, however the Home Office could.

Generally speaking I have a excellent relationship with my consultant and this in turn meant I could confide in her any secrets I had, and although she was not pleased with what I was doing, again, like my mother, she understood I could not survive on the benefits system. It was obvious my doctor was not happy with my line of work but I was honest with her, even if she could see pitfalls that I could not.

Other people who thought it was a great lad's job were the lads from the pub. Constantly I used to get asked if I got any freebies, or failing that did I get staff discount. It was almost like I was becoming a bit of a celebrity footballer, but to me it was just a job and a way to make ends meet. I was not in the job for the kudos, but to be honest I did enjoy the work. In some ways I became a bit of an agony uncle to some of the ladies I worked with. One occasion I found myself helping Pamela to find a new house that she had been offered by the council. On another occasion one of the ladies asked me to attend a hospital appointment with her for a smear test, as she did not want to go on her own. Other things I would do would be maybe to drive someone to the local Butlins with their children when they booked a holiday, and then pick them up at the end of the week. Nina was another girl who was with us for a short time. On one night I got into trouble because when I dropped her off after a job I spent the next half an hour giving her careers advice. Her boyfriend at the time thought there was something going on and so he rang The Boss and although she wasn't that bothered, she did give me a bit of an ear roasting.

Chapter 9

Around eight months into the job I was becoming quite close to The Boss. Initially when I worked for her The Boss kept me at arm's length. I was just another employee. However, we became quite close and it would not be uncommon for The Boss to invite me in for a coffee when I was dropping her takings off. At this point a lot of the agency girls had come and gone. This included Ella who had moved on when she found a boyfriend. I wouldn't say I was sad about seeing Ella go. However, I did miss her because she was funny and one of the easiest to work with. No more would we spend nights at McDonalds talking and making each other laugh. She had moved on in her life and that was fair enough - although now and then we would both bump into each other in Hessle where we lived. The Boss, however, was not going anywhere and I was beginning to earn The Boss's confidence. I did know her ex-husband and as far as I could tell we were still mates. The Boss was becoming less of a boss and more of a mate.

I was round at The Boss's house one night nursing a coffee and she told me it was her anniversary today. The agency had been running for exactly 21 years. It was then when it struck me that The Boss must have been around 19 or 20 when she started the agency. The Boss had worked the London circuit for several of the top London agencies. She went on to tell me she could earn up to £2000 a night and stay in some of the top hotels with wealthy Arab clients. Also, the agency she worked for expected the girls to be slim, trim and well turned out at all times. They would even weigh some of the girls to make sure none of them put any weight on. The Boss certainly knew how to spin a yarn and some of the stories she told me were fascinating. For whatever reason, she moved up to Hull in her early twenties and opened the agency. From there she never looked back. However, The Boss did have her issues. She was trying to get clean from drugs. Although she was not doing too badly, occasionally she would relapse every six months. It was a shame and I felt sorry for her.

I had a lot of time for The Boss. She was tough when she needed to be, sometimes with me, but she never took any shit off any of the girls. She knew how to make money but she was never arrogant with it. The Boss looked after me every time I did a job and even if I picked her up to run her to Hull station, The Boss always paid handsomely even though I would have done the job for nothing. More than this though, The Boss always had my back. On one occasion, Julie was being bothered by her neighbour who was making Julie's life a misery. When I confided this to The Boss she offered to send a girl round (whose name I can't remember) in order to fill-in this neighbour. From what I could gather this person was a big butch dyke that didn't often hit women and preferred to fight men. The boss was more than happy to look after her workers when she needed to. Unfortunately down the line, The Boss and I would come to fall out. Although, when I worked for her I regarded her as one of my best mates.

Chapter 10

Part of the job was always to make sure that I had condoms in the car. Again, with the cutbacks, the local clinic where I normally got the condoms from decided that I had to go to a separate place to get protection. It was the same type of thing, but a privately-run company, subsidised by the government. Unfortunately, however, the condoms that they gave me were useless. A few of the girls told me that the protection that they were using had split, so I had to source condoms from somewhere else. But this wasn't a problem in itself. I sent a round-robin text to all the girls, including The Boss, telling them all to disregard the condoms that I had given them, as they were ineffective and I would source some protection from elsewhere.

One or two texted back, basically saying the same thing; they'd all had the experience of them breaking. Soon, however, I received a text from Tiffany - she needed to see me and she wanted to talk. It was a Sunday afternoon and I picked her up and asked her if she wanted a drink at mine. When we got to my house I offered her a cup of tea, however she said that she would prefer a beer. As I handed her the cold can of Fosters I asked what the problem was and what she needed to talk about. It could have been anything. Maybe she was pregnant, maybe she had family problems. Did she want to leave the agency and not know how to tell The Boss?

Initially, she was reluctant to talk. She finished her can, then turned to me and said, "I've got a crush on you".

There was not a lot that I could say, really. And I knew that both Tiffany and I could lose our jobs if I'd mentioned it to The Boss. In the end, we had another drink and I took her home.

Chapter 11

It wasn't unusual for the agency to be asked for special requests. In fact, it was quite common for wives to ring up to book a threesome with a "bi" girl for the husband's birthday. Most, but not all, of the girls on the books were bi-sexual. Also, on other occasions, wives would ring up to book an escort for their husbands. For example, if the husband or boyfriend was staying at a hotel in Hull on business. It was almost as if the wives in question were pleased with the break. Then there were other fantasies that we catered for. Obviously, the clients would ring for threesomes with two ladies. Other clients would ring wanting to engage in "water sports" - although not all of the ladies that I worked with were happy to do this. I remember one occasion when a guy from East Hull rang up and his fantasy was for an escort to go around and pretend that he was a giant baby. This particular job was done by Angel and although there was an extra charge for the service, I could tell when Angel came out of the job that even she, an experienced escort, found it a bit taxing. Not only did she have to bath him, but she also had to dry him off, put a towel on him as a pretend nappy and then rock him in her arms and sing to him.

Other fantasies that were common included rubber gloves. Some of the clients liked to watch girls smoking, whilst another client in particular liked nothing more than to be covered in baby oil.

One job that I particularly remember was with Melissa. Melissa was a nymphomaniac and loved her job. This particular night I had to take Melissa to a house in Cottingham and The Boss left me strict instructions not to leave her. I pulled into the cul-de-sac, not far from the village centre, and in this particular house were five guys and Melissa had to entertain them all. Not only that, but the job went on for five hours. I remember falling asleep at the wheel but trying to stay awake and alert in case there was a problem, only for Melissa to come out at 6 a.m. with a shitload of money and a big smile on her face. She then played it down, saying that all she had to do was talk.

Chapter 12

There was one escort in particular that all the girls hated, although I didn't have a problem with her per se. It was not uncommon for the girls to bitch about each other in between jobs. However, all were adamant that they didn't like Cassie. Cassie was in her mid-twenties with long dark hair and very attractive, but she could also be very cold. From what I could gather, Cassie had not had the easiest start in life. However, soon after she started working for the agency Cassie enrolled at College and spent the next two and a half years studying accountancy. But more than this, she left full-time education without any debt. However, Cassie was one of the most popular girls on our books and it wasn't uncommon for her to do several jobs a night. This was probably one of the reasons that the other girls hated her so much. Most of the ladies that I worked with would talk about their jobs when they got in the car, even if they weren't supposed to. For example; whether it was a good job or a bad job; whether the client was kind, respectful and warm or whether they were living in a shithole with empty takeaway boxes all over the house, as well as beer cans; whether they kept good hygiene or not. Generally, the girls would talk. Cassie, however, was different - almost cold and detached.

However, there was one occasion when I saw a different side to Cassie. It was about nine o'clock one summer's evening when I was taking Cassie home from a job. I was just driving over Marfleet Bridge when I happened to notice in the corner of my eye a young girl, no more than six or seven years old, in her pyjamas with nothing on her feet and although it was still light I commented to Cassie "Look at that! A bairn out at this time of night, on her own!". Immediately, Cassie made me stop the car. We pulled up alongside the little girl and Cassie tried talking to her. She asked her her name. However, the little girl did not respond. Again, Cassie tried to engage with the little girl, even telling her her real name. The little girl was obviously frightened and scared, so we rang the police in order for the little girl to be taken care of. I could tell that Cassie could empathise with her - Cassie had been through the same sort of shit. When the police came I gave them my name and address and told them that I was just taking my girlfriend back home. I dropped Cassie off at her flat, however by this time the same old Cassie had returned. A defensive wall had come up and she was hiding her emotions again. Cassie was one tough bitch.

Chapter 13

It was a slow night and there wasn't much doing. I think I'd done just one job all night when The Boss rang and asked me to pick up Angel. I picked her up from her house in Sutton and made my way towards Beverley Road in Hull. As soon as Angel got in the car she said, "I've got a bad feeling about this job". I asked her what she meant. And again she said, "Just that I've got a bad feeling about this job".

Angel was quite a spiritualist and regularly did tarot readings. However, on this particular night she was uneasy. I told her that she didn't have to do it, and that if she wanted I could take her home, at which point she fired back at me, "Oh yeah, The Boss will love that - if I don't turn up to a job that I'm on my way to".

The job itself should have been quite simple. It was two guys who wanted Angel for half-an hour each, in separate rooms. As soon as I got to the job, on a shitty little cul-de-sac off Beverley Road I turned the car around to face the direction that I would be leaving and pulled up outside the client's house. It was then that I reassured Angel that I would not be going anywhere and that I'd be outside when the job was over. She got out of the car and I just noticed this small black face open the door to her as she went inside.

I'd literally just picked up the book that I was reading when the phone rang. It was The Boss, "Robbo there's a problem. Get her out of there".

I asked The Boss to elaborate what the problem was, just for my own peace of mind. She said that Angel wasn't happy because there were four guys in there. "Okay, leave it with me" I reassured The Boss and I made my way to the front door. I could see one of the black guys as well as Angel, through the frosted glass on the front door. I tried the front door handle but the door was locked, so I slammed my fist against the wooden door frame and saw this black figure almost jump out of his skin. After ten seconds the door had still not been opened, so I banged furiously again, against the door. As the dark figure approached from behind the glass, I braced myself in case he was holding a weapon. A small weaselly Bangladeshi guy appeared from behind the door. However I could see nobody else except Angel stood at the bottom of the stairs.

My first concerns were for Angel, and I asked her what the problem was. She told me that there were only supposed to be two guys, however there were four in the property and, she added, "One looks about fourteen. He's old enough to be my son. I'm not fucking doing it". At this point, the Bangladeshi guy held up his arms in protest and said, "You can't do this to him. You can't do this to him". At the same time The Boss rang, "Robbo, once you get Angel in the car, get the call-out fee". I was beginning to get stressed at this point. I turned the phone off and put it in my pocket, at which point I turned to Angel and said, "Get in the car, now!". Like a soldier following an order, Angel made straight for the door and I stepped aside so that she could get into the car, then I turned to the Bangladeshi guy, "Right. I need the thirty quid call-out fee". At which point he began shaking his head and began to mutter in a heavily-accented voice, "I don't understand". I reiterated the fact that I needed the call-out fee and again he played ignorant, claiming that he did not understand. I watched Angel get into my car and I thought for a second. The Boss had plenty of enforcers who could do her work - I wasn't here for that, my priority was looking after the girls. If that meant leaving a job without being paid, as long as the girl was safe, then so be it. I turned to the Bangladeshi guy and said "Someone will be here soon, to collect what you owe" and with that I shut the door, climbed into my car and took Angel home.

Chapter 14

It was a Saturday night and I'd just finished a job over in East Hull. Again,

I was working the phones this particular night when a text came through. It read, "Is Lily available tonight, for an hour?"

I replied that she was available. I got the address and reassured the client that I would be there within the next half an hour. The job was on Caroline Place, near Hull city centre and fortunately it was not far from where Lily lived. Lily was in her mid-fifties, was overweight and, to be honest, was past it. However, she was a pleasant enough lady and I never had any problems working with her. Soon after I picked her up we were at the job on Caroline Place. I told Lily that I was doing the phones that night and to ring me for the "safe and happy". She got out of her car and made her way to the job. Five minutes had passed and there was still no call. Again, this wasn't unusual, so I decided to remain patient for a few more minutes. It was at this point that I saw Lily walking back to the car.

As she got inside I could tell that she was not happy, and she just said, "He said that I wasn't his type and that he didn't want me".

I replied, "Did you get the call-out fee?"

"No," she answered, "he just shut the door".

I stepped out of the car and made my way to the client's door. He had specifically asked for Lily so one could only assume that he knew what he was getting. I slammed on the door and initially there was no answer. However, I persevered and eventually a weedy looking man in his fifties answered. I tried my best not to laugh as this guy was dressed as a caveman. I told him that I needed the call out fee and he wasn't happy. Also, I could smell whisky on his breath. Initially, he refused to pay so I explained to him that if he refused to pay that he would be blacklisted from the agency and we wouldn't be sending girls to him again. This infuriated him even more and he started going on about how he was a Middlesbrough lad and how he "knew people" and this wouldn't happen up there. I stood my ground and eventually he handed over the call out fee. However, it was hard not to laugh at him, dressed as "Captain Caveman".

I went back to the car and handed Lily her share of the call out fee. She just added, "He was a creep and a weirdo anyway". Soon, I dropped her off at home. Captain Caveman went on to make a complaint with The Boss, but again, The Boss backed me up. The fact that the client had specifically asked for Lily meant that it was the client's mistake. Therefore, if he did not like the look of her when she arrived then it was only fair that he paid the call out fee.

However, again, it did ring true how potentially dangerous my job could be. Captain Caveman could have been armed or there could have been a gang of men in his flat. It just brought home the reality of the world that I was working in - it wouldn't be the last time.

It was the early hours of Sunday morning when a job came in for Tiffany on Greatfield Estate in East Hull. Greatfield Estate itself is not a place you want to be at any time. Half past two on a Sunday morning and the red flags were flying in my mind. We found the job easy enough and the house was in the middle of the regeneration projects – so, therefore, some houses were boarded up waiting to be demolished. On this particular street there was about three houses that were not boarded up and Tiffany went to one of them.

I was doing the phones again this night and as soon as Tiffany got in I received the "safe and happy". As I sat there after about twenty minutes a car pulled up along the street and there were two very dodgy looking men sat in the front. I noticed the death stare as they drove past. I watched in the mirror as the car braked but then within a minute it drove off. Not long later the car returned and, again, as it passed me from behind I felt the death stares from both of these guys. The car then pulled up in front of me, turned round and pulled up alongside me. At this point, given the nature of the work, I always carried a can of deicer along the side of the seat. As the window of the other car came down to talk to me, I removed the cap of the deicer. Both men looked angry and curious. One of them certainly looked like he was on something. "Who are you looking for" said the driver. I had to think fast. "What you doing here". It would be easy to say "mind your own business" but that would not have defused the situation. These guys were obviously drug dealing and they didn't know whether I was an undercover copper, or someone dealing on their patch. All this happened in seconds. I told them who I worked for and the name of the company and I added that I was just waiting for one of our girls to finish the job. I didn't know if they were going to believe me or not. Both men looked at each other and both smiled, then turned to me and said "no problem mate" then the druggie added, "just watch yourself round here, it can be dodgy on a night." After that the car drove off into the night and I replaced the cap on the deicer.

Chapter 15

I was in the pub one afternoon when I received a call from a very stressed out Summer. As I said earlier, it wasn't uncommon for me to receive these calls, usually when the girls needed a lift or someone to talk to. This time Summer was almost crying. "Robbo, I am being blackmailed". I asked her to explain and the upshot was, a friend of hers from the gym, probably someone who fancied her, had lent Summer some money. Not quite a four-figure sum, but a significant amount. Summer earlier had confided in him what she was doing for work and initially it wasn't a problem. However, when his advances were rejected by Summer, he decided he wanted his money back. From this point the relationship went sour, so in the end this individual claimed he would tell Summer's parent what she was doing unless she paid him the money. This could cause a problem for all concerned.

Summer gave me the guy's number and I rang him. He seemed taken aback that he had received this call from me, but in the end we agreed that if Summer paid him, nothing more needs to happen. I called Summer back and I explained to her that the best option was to just pay him off. In hindsight, I think Summer thought that if I put the squeeze on this guy she wouldn't have to pay him, and although this was an option, the best option all round would be to pay the guy on the understanding that he remained quiet. This was the best solution and the upshot was Summer paid him in full – problem solved.

I told The Boss about that afternoon's drama and The Boss was not happy with Summer. The Boss did not want attention bringing to the business. However, The Boss was happy that it was dealt with and I think I earned a few brownie points with The Boss.

Another problem which arose was with one of the new drivers,

Mohammed. I am not entirely sure which country Mohammed came from and his main job was delivering pizzas but when his shift finished, he worked for us as a second driver. Things were going fine with Mohammed at first and I would regularly go to see him to take The Boss's takings. He had a flat down Willerby Road where he lived with his heavily pregnant wife. Soon after his baby son was born, however, it became apparent he was taking advantage of the girls. This only came to light when Pamela told me what he had been doing. I had a word with one or two of the other girls and they all said the same. I explained to Pamela I had to tell The Boss. Pamela at this point thought she would be in trouble, but I explained to her that if it wasn't nipped in the bud, then it could lead to a problem later down the line. Pamela went on to say that Mohammed was all over her on some nights and would use the excuse that since his wife had had the baby, he didn't get any sex at home. The upshot was Mohammed was soon sacked. What was funny was he had tried the same thing with Cassie and he even asked her "how much do you want for 15 minutes". Cassie was calm and collective, almost to the point of coldness and she replied "I don't do 15 minutes".

Chapter 16

One of the clients we regularly serviced was a blind guy who lived in the centre of town. By all accounts he was a nice guy, even if he was a bit naive. On several occasions when we arrived at the job, he would ask me to come with him to the cash point although more often than not this was pre-arranged with the office. We would drive from his house to the cash point in St Stephen's, a large shopping centre in the middle of Hull, and we would literally walk with this guy to the cash point and he would ask us to put in his pin. On some occasions I had to do it, but mostly it was the girls who looked after him. Most of the girls could be trusted, but certainly not all of them. On the last occasion I told him to have his money ready and I explained to him that although the girls were happy to oblige his needs, it could lead to a problem if we had a new girl that we didn't know if we could trust her or not and it was in his interest to have the money ready.

Taking clients to cash points was also part of the job sometimes, although I wasn't always comfortable doing it. I would always make sure the client got in the front with the escort on the back seat. The reason for this was simple, I didn't know if they were going to attack me, so it was easier to deal with if they were in the front. One evening I did a job with Cassie at the Village Hotel in Hessle, the client was an Australian and he kept on bragging about how he used to be a porn star and how he used to be a male escort himself. Cassie and I just nodded and agreed, even though it was obvious to both of us that the client was talking out of his arse. The reason for this was simple; there is no market for it. I would often get asked in the pub whether there were any male escorts on the books and particularly the young lads would say "I would make a great escort". The fact was that if a woman wanted to get off with someone, she wouldn't ring an escort agency to do it. She would probably get dolled up and go to the pub, and this was the reason The Boss didn't have any men on her books.

I would regularly have the radio on whilst in the car. Some of the girls were rockers, like me, loved nothing more than listening to AC/DC or Black Sabbath in between jobs, but most, if not all, of the girls were into the music. One song I constantly remember was the George Michael hit Father Figure, and I would often go home to return to this song whilst watching on You Tube. What made the song more poignant was the video in which George Michael plays a taxi driver, driving a model across the City.

Some of the girls on the books were like models and listening to the music video, I could relate to the character in the video.

Chapter 17

The boss and I were not getting on. There were two reasons for this. Firstly, I was getting a bit tired of the job. This was no surprise as I had done nearly 17 months, seven days a week, with only the odd night off in between. The other reason we were not getting on was because The Boss was using again. For some reason Paul was back on the books as a driver and I could not help but notice Paul was getting more work than me. One of the reasons for this was because Paul would do the drug runs whereas I completely refused to have anything to do with drugs, it was against my religion. I had mentioned to one or two of the girls that I was getting fed up and this was obviously feeding back to The Boss. One night whilst I was on a job, The Boss and I had a massive argument and it was obvious that she was coming down. She had recently been in hospital and as such had had her morphine reduced and even though I visited her in hospital and was running the company whilst she was ill, I felt that this was not being appreciated by The Boss.

Things came to a head one night when a new girl started. I was still fuming from the argument and I said more than I should have done to the new girl. This included personal things that The Boss had confided in me, although I don't think it is appropriate to disclose them now. The long and the short of it was that the new girl told everything I had told her to The Boss. Obviously The Boss was livid. The next night was a Saturday and I decided a week before that I was going to have a night out with my band The Jackdaws. Again, because The Boss was out of her head, she did not realise that I had booked the night off until the Saturday morning and even though I had booked it well in advance, The Boss was not happy.

That night I met up with the band in the pub and it wasn't long after when I started getting the calls and texts from The Boss. These were basically saying she needed the work's phone as well as the takings for that week. Because I was still angry with her, I told The Boss in no uncertain terms that "she would not be getting the phone or the money tonight." I was on a night out and I was determined to let my hair down.

After a fantastic night out, I woke up the next afternoon with a massive hangover and there were about seven missed calls from The Boss. Once I had woken up properly and I had had my fix of two coffees, I made my call and The Boss told me she needed the phone and the money straight away. It was looking increasingly likely that I was going to be sacked, but to be honest I was past caring. Soon I drove to The Boss's and when I pulled up outside her house, she came straight out and sat in the car. It was at this point she took the phone and the money off me. Then she proceeded to interrogate me about what I had said to the new girl. At this point I was still suffering from a hangover, so all my responses were short and flippant. The Boss got out of my car and slammed my door. At which point, I put the car in reverse and made my way back to Hessle. It was obvious I had lost my job, but again I was past caring. The job was starting to wear me down. Not least because of the impact when you told people what you did for a living. Being a minder for an escort agency is not something you wish to disclose at a wine tasting or cocktail party and, although the money was good and part of me enjoyed the work, I felt that it had run its course. I hoped that that would be the end of it.

Chapter 18

Within a week of leaving, I received my first phone call from Lenny. Lenny was a guy The Boss knew who was in prison and by all accounts, a very undesirable creature. Initially, he said "why are you bothering my sister." Even though The Boss had met Lenny in a crack house in London, a kinship had developed between the two and The Boss always referred to Lenny as her brother. However, Lenny was now doing serious time for allegedly raping an old age pensioner, although both Lenny and The Boss had both protested his innocence. Lenny was known for armed robbery and by all accounts was a nuisance. However, the Boss claimed that he was stitched up by the Met Police.

When I got the call from Lenny, initially I told him that I had been good to The Boss and that I had gone out of my way to help her with her addiction, as well as running the company. With that Lenny seemed to take on board what I was saying. Then he told me "look I am sorry for bothering you." With that I then texted The Boss and told her in no uncertain terms "there were to be no more calls from Lenny." This in turn turned out to be a tit for tat. The Boss decided to get clever and to get Lenny to call me again. The conversation wasn't as amicable this time. Both of us were shouting at each other and in the end I told him "If you're coming for me, you best be good, I've served in both the Infantry and the Paras and I have done SAS selection and I've killed bigger and nastier men than you will ever be. If you come after me, I'm going to come after all of you, so the best thing you can do is leave me alone." Like I said it became a bit of a tit for tat, almost my dad is bigger than your dad. It wasn't long before the police got involved.

I had taken Julie away for the weekend to Robin Hood's Bay for a well-earned break. By all accounts we had a fantastic and relaxing time and I could afford to do it with some of the money I had saved from work. We were driving back Sunday afternoon when I got the call from a PC Love. The Boss had rung the police claiming that I was harassing her girls. Only four days earlier I had rung the police to report threatening calls from Lenny. However, for some reason the police had not followed up and were not investigating my claim. Now the boot was on the other foot and The Boss had made a complaint.

I got to Beverley Police Station and saw PC Love. Not only this, I had shown her all the messages from The Boss and Lenny on my phone and the Officer soon realised The Boss had an agenda. I explained to PC Love about The Boss's drug usage, the threatening calls from Lenny and that I had reported it to the police but they had taken no action. It was at this point I remembered The Boss claiming she had connections with the police force. The Officer could not understand, or could certainly not explain, why when I had made a complaint it was not acted upon or certainly taken seriously. However, she also saw that The Boss was also making claims that were unjustifiable. The upshot was both The Boss and I received a reprimand to keep away from each other and not to contact each other.

Later that afternoon, I told my mother what had happened with the police and with The Boss and I had shown mum the messages that were on my phone. They were worded in such a way that it was obvious, mum said, that The Boss had someone telling her what to say and again it gave credence to the fact that The Boss had someone high up in the police who was covering for her.

Later that night, I went to see Jeremy, the vicar who had married Julie and me, and I explained to him everything that had gone on and we both sat there in his office and said a prayer for all concerned. I am not sure if this made any real difference but I felt a lot calmer after I had left. There was only one person left to see after this and that was my old boss.

Fred lived in the villages and was a former SAS soldier. I had always turned to Fred when I needed advice on certain things and by all accounts Fred told me how it was every time. I explained to Fred about how The

Boss had contacts within the police, as well as everything else that had gone on. His advice was to go to my local MP, Alan Johnson. Within six months of talking to Fred, Humberside Police Chief Constable had resigned. I was not to know whether this was as a result of what had gone on or not, but by all accounts I had no more trouble.

Chapter 19

A lot of the girls left after I was sacked. From what I can gather, Cassie in particular had created hell with The Boss and refused to work with Paul and made it clear The Boss was to reinstate me. Other girls left as well, although I kept in touch with one or two. One still cuts my hair; another girl had left the company just before me to be with her boyfriend. However, they had broken up and she found herself homeless. She had been sofa surfing for some time when the council managed to get her a flat. However, she had no furniture of any description and it turned out the ex-boyfriend had even burnt all her clothes. With some of the money I had left from working, I decorated her flat and got her the essentials, such as a bed and a washing machine – although we are not in touch today.

After a few months Cassie got in touch and she was working independently, usually on a weekend. She asked me if I would drive for her now and again and to be fair she paid me well. However, more recently I would get hysterical texts from Cassie, sometimes three or four in the space of a minute. In one text she asked me if I would kill her. It was obvious Cassie was becoming unwell. I did my best to try and get het the help she needed, but unfortunately Cassie took this the wrong way and asked me not to contact her again.

Lastly, I still see Ella, if only occasionally, in the pub or when she walks her dog. We exchange pleasantries but both our lives have moved on significantly now.

Three Years Later

I have not heard from or contacted The Boss for some time. In fact I did not even know if the company was still running as the website was out of date and unsecure. I wanted so much to make peace with The Boss, so I rang her out of the blue. The conversation was a little slow at first but ultimately I wanted to apologise for how we fell out. Initially, when The Boss received the call she was on the defensive and I could tell she was probably recording the conversation. However, ultimately she apologised to me as well. A certain understanding had developed between us and hopefully a future peace.

Within a few days I received a call from The Boss again. This time she wanted me to drive for her, only I was to drive her "friends" from Leeds around the city. It could not have been more obvious what The Boss was involved in now and I was having no part of it. Like I had said earlier, "it was against my religion." I politely declined the offer.

Working as a minder for an escort agency was a good job and I enjoyed it. Even the boring nights when you are sat in a freezing cold car in the middle of winter was better than sitting at home on the dole. Also I enjoyed the interaction with the girls. I certainly hope everyone I worked with are getting on with their lives and are happy. As for the moral justification for what I was doing, at the end of the day I was security for the girls doing a dangerous job and I liked to think I did the job well. Not only protecting the girls but respectful as well. As for The Boss, I bear her no ill will, in fact I hope she is clean and doing o.k. The fact was she was a fantastic boss.

There is a song that I listen to quite regularly which reminds me of the time I was working as a minder. It is by a guy called Bobby Womack entitled Across 110th Street. This seems to sum up what it was like working in those times. Check it out - you may see where I am coming from. As for any repercussions for writing this book, I can't see there being many. After all, there are things that I have left out and will continue to do so as long as I don't get any hassle. I know where the bodies are buried.

Printed in Great Britain
by Amazon